How to Pre
Words for Worship in Print and on Screen

Mark Earey

Director of Anglican Formation and Tutor in Liturgy, The Queen's Foundation for Ecumenical Theological Education, Birmingham and Member of the Church of England Liturgical Commission

GROVE BOOKS LIMITED

RIDLEY HALL RD CAMBRIDGE CB3 9HU

Contents

Acknowledgments

Some of the material in this booklet has been adapted from my earlier book, 'Producing Your Own Orders of Service' (Church House Publishing, 2000). I am grateful to the publishers for permission to reuse some of this material.

I would like to thank the Group for Renewal of Worship for bearing with my obsessions about this topic (and even sharing some of them). They have made many suggestions for improvement, and I would like to especially thank Anna de Lange, Colin Buchanan, Graham Hunter, Anne Harrison, John Leach, Charles Read, Andy Stinson and Ian Tarrant for taking time to offer detailed suggestions.

First Impression May 2021
ISSN 0144-1728
ISBN 978 1 78827 161 5

1
Why Bother?

Corporate worship should bring honour and praise to God, and should help those taking part to keep their focus on God without being distracted or confused by the practicalities.

Christians have always known this, and that is why those involved in the worship of the church have always sought to offer God their best. That means, in some traditions, that care is taken to keep the brass polished and the clerical robes ironed, and the flower arrangers aim to do their very best. It means that we try to make sure that the church noticeboard is clear and accurate, as well as attractive, and so is the church website. In other traditions it means taking care that the interior of the church looks modern and welcoming, that the coffee is top quality, and the audio and video facilities would not look out of place in a conference centre—'professional' in the best sense of the word.

This booklet is about another aspect of that desire for corporate worship to honour God and to help the worshippers to stay focused: the words that enable worship to take place, both sung and spoken. Whether we are providing those words in print or on screen (either in person or online), they need to help the congregation to worship. They should be easy to follow and accurate in content. They should not be so attractive in style that they demand attention themselves, or so poorly presented that they leave worshippers unsure how to take part, and distract them from the focus on God. Like other aspects of corporate worship, they should demonstrate a concern for accessibility, including an awareness of the needs of those who have visual impairment, dyslexia, learning disabilities or who are new to reading.

Whether you are preparing the words for a printed order of service, a PowerPoint presentation for in-church Sunday worship, or material for an online service, there should be one thing in common—no one should notice how the words are presented. When we get it right, worshippers are clear about what they say or sing, are helped to participate and understand and, more importantly, are enabled to focus on God. When we get it wrong, however, our congregations find themselves less able to worship God—though they might not always notice *why*.

Print and Screen

As you come to this booklet, you probably have a particular need in mind. More and more, this need is focused on words on screen—either projected or displayed on screens in church buildings or, increasingly, displayed on screens in people's hands or homes as they join in online worship. Other churches will still be focused on paper resources, both for in-church services and for worship at home.

Even in churches that primarily use screens for regular worship, there are times when printed material is needed. This might include printed resources for those who cannot see the screen, perhaps because of impaired vision or because they cannot stand for long periods. But there are also other instances when printed material might be necessary, such as a large-print service leaflet and / or hymn sheet for worship in a care home, or a song sheet for outdoor carol-singing. There are occasions when the printed order of service becomes an important keepsake or record of what took place—for instance, a wedding, a funeral, the welcoming of a new minister or a service marking an historic event or anniversary.

Print and screen will both be needed in our worship for the foreseeable future, even if in most churches the balance will tend to favour one over the other. This booklet aims to improve practice in local churches ,whichever medium is used. It might be useful for your own practice—or it might be that you need to buy a copy for some other people who play key roles in getting the words for worship to the worshippers each week.

Though we will touch on topics to do with screens, PowerPoint, liturgy, technology, accessibility and online worship, these are not dealt with in detail. For more on some of these issues, see the following:

Shayne Ardron et al, *Learning from Lockdown* (Grove Worship booklet W246) for more on online worship.

Ian Tarrant, *How to Worship with Data Projection: PowerPoint and Other Tools* (W192) for more on screens in worship.

Mark Earey, *How to Use Words Well: Key Skills for Worship Leaders* (W231) for guidance about writing and choosing liturgical texts.

Katie Tupling and Anna de Lange, *Worship and Disability: A Kingdom for All* (W235) for more on accessibility.

Helen Bent and Liz Tipple, *Worship 4 Today—Part 3* (London: CHP, 2014) pp 27–40 for more on using screens and technology.

2

Word Processing Tips

This chapter is focused on techniques that can help you get the most out of word processor or slideshow software. Some of what follows is really basic. Some of it is a bit more sophisticated. Some of it applies primarily for printed orders of service; other tips are just as important for words on screen.

Even if you have been using word processors for years, there just might be a nugget of new information hidden in here, so do not skip ahead too soon...

> **Jargon: 'Font'**
>
> I use the term 'fonts' to refer to different typefaces (such as Arial, Times New Roman, Verdana). This is the term which is used by most software. It is not to be confused with the other kind, used for baptism!

Only Put One Space Between Sentences

Typewriters needed two spaces between sentences, and so those of a particular generation still tend to put two spaces in. On a modern computer the letters are proportionally spaced and sit closer together, so each word is more distinct. This makes it easy to tell where the gaps are between sentences and so we do not *need* two spaces any more. In fact two spaces makes it look as if the sentences are not on speaking terms, and leaves big white gaps in blocks of text.

Margin And Column Settings

Many word processors assume that a new document is always going to be a letter, and they set the default margins accordingly. For most printed orders of service, a margin of about 1 cm will be right.

If you are using two columns (for instance, to make a folded leaflet from an A4 sheet), make sure you set a wide enough gap between columns. If you are using 1 cm margins, you need a column spacing of 2 cm for a folded leaflet.

> **Jargon: 'Points'**
>
> The vertical size of print is measured in points. There are 72 points to 1 inch.

Learn to Use Styles

Most word processors allow you to allocate pre-set styles to text. These enable you to make changes to the whole document with just a couple of clicks (for instance, to see what happens if you make the congregational text larger, or if you change the font).

Set up a different style for each type of text you use regularly (Heading; Congregation; Leader; Instructions; Hymn/ Song; Source/Acknowledgement).

> **Headings and Titles**
>
> *Instructions and other non-spoken words.*
>
> Words for the leader to say.
> **Words for the congregation to say.**
>
> Indented text for a hymn or a song,
> *And further indented, and in italic,*
> *for the chorus or refrain.*
> *Copyright & source info*

For each style you can set font, size, alignment, spacing, bold/italic and so on.

Use paragraph settings to help. For instance, set the leader's text to have no spacing after the paragraph, and the congregation's text to have 6-point spacing after the paragraph. This way, the leader's cue lines will be kept with the congregation's response, with a gap before the next leader's line.

> **Practical Tip: Slideshow Styles**
>
> Slideshow software does not always have provision for setting styles, but you can achieve similar effects by editing the slide master, and setting defaults for font, size, and effects for different levels of text.

Set a Template

Most word processor or slideshow software allows you to save a document or slideshow as a template so that you can use it as the basis for every new service. It is worth spending some time setting up a template with settings that work for the worship context, such as margins, column sizes, fonts and styles for different sorts of text.

Use Line Breaks

A line break (sometimes known as a soft return) allows you to break a line without starting a new paragraph. You can put in a line break by pressing SHIFT + RETURN at the end of the line, rather than RETURN.

Using line breaks means that a whole prayer, or the whole verse of a song or hymn, will be treated as one paragraph. You can therefore change the whole block by clicking anywhere within it and applying the change. It also means that if you have set automatic spacing at the end of paragraphs of a particular type, they will not get put in after every line.

Turn Off Automatic Capitalization

Some software will try to correct your work by automatically putting the first letter of a new line in capitals. This can be very unhelpful when you are typing in a prayer or a song, where a new line does not necessarily start a new sentence. Find the setting and turn it off.

Use Turnovers, Not Hyphens

If a sentence is too long to fit on one line, use an indented turnover. This is when you put in a line break at a sensible point, and then indent the rest of the sentence on the next line to show that the sentence continues.

Use an indented turnover like this:

As we forgive those
** who trespass against us.**

And do not hyphenate like this:

As we forgive those who tres-
pass against us.

If you let the software break the sentence, it might not do it in the best place, and it might even split a word by hyphenating it, so make sure you turn off the auto-hyphenation feature.

Practical Tip: Turnovers

Because turnovers have to be introduced manually, they do not change when you make other changes to the text (changing font size, for instance) and so special care is needed at the proofreading stage to make sure they are still appropriate.

Avoid Underlining

Underlining was a great way of adding emphasis to handwritten or typewritten text, but nowadays it tends to look rather old-fashioned. It also makes text harder to read, because the underline cuts through the descenders of letters (the parts that go beneath the line, like the tail on a g, p or q).

If you want to make a heading stand out, use bold, a different font, a larger size or a different text alignment.

Practical Tip: Importing Text with a Different Format

If you are pasting text into your presentation or order of service that has come from another document or from the internet, it is likely to be a different font, different size or different line-spacing. This can wreck your carefully prepared layout. When you paste the text in, the secret is to select the paste option, 'Keep text only' (rather than options to use the source or destination formatting). This way the bare text will take on whatever formatting you have at that point in your receiving document.

Basic Good Practice

3

How Much Text to Include

A really important starting point is to decide whether to give the congregation the same text as the leader, or to focus on the bits that they need.

Full Text (All the Leader's Words as Well as the Congregation's)

- This makes things clear for the congregation, but it also restricts the leader's opportunity to be flexible or spontaneous. It can be very confusing (especially for visitors) if the leader is saying one thing but the text on paper or screen suggests they will be saying something else.
- Some people like to follow the leader's words.
- Full text can be helpful for people with hearing impairment.

Congregational Text Only

- This allows for greater flexibility in the leader's words.
- Takes up less space.
- Encourages people to engage visually in the action, rather than burying their heads in a printed text or looking in another direction at a screen.
- Some people find it confusing to have some of the words printed, but not all of them.
- It means you will probably need to produce a separate full-text edition for leaders and musicians.

If you decide only to include the congregation's words, make sure that you give some instructions which make clear what will happen in between (for instance, '*The leader continues the prayer*'). This will help the congregation to be ready to come in with their part.

Also, make sure you give the leader's cue lines which lead into the congregational text. Remember that ellipses (three dots:...) can be used to show that there is text missed out, or that the person leading is expected to add extra material (for instance, some specific points in prayers of intercession).

Do Not Forget Headings

Headings help to show the shape and structure of the service and make the journey through the service easier to follow. This applies on screen as well as in print.

In a printed order of service, they also make it easier to direct people to the right place.

For Print—Page Orientation

There are two basic options if you are using A4 size paper:

A4 folded to A5	• Spacious layout with lots of white space • Room for pictures, if needed • Works well for booklets of several pages • Good when you need space for a margin (such as to indicate who says particular lines—bride, candidate, sponsor etc) • Longer lines can remain unbroken even at larger font sizes • Not the most efficient use of paper • Good for a booklet for regular use
A4 folded long-ways	• Less spacious feel • Most efficient use of paper (because most lines of prayers and songs are about the right length to fit) • Works well for a leaflet (one sheet of paper) or short booklet—not so good for a longer booklet • No space for margins • Good for a one-off form of service or those used less frequently

However, there might be other factors to consider, such as the size or shape of your pew shelves or equivalent. The service leaflet might keep falling off if it is the wrong shape, and this could constrain your choice.

Rookie Error: A4 Landscape Threefold

An A4 sheet folded into three is also a very efficient use of paper, but it is quite easy to get lost after the front page. Best avoided if possible.

Text Style

Serif Or Sans Serif Font?

Serif fonts look more traditional—*eg* Times New Roman. The serifs are the little flicks at the ends of letters. The thickness of the lines in each letter varies—parts will be thick and other parts thin.

Sans serif fonts look more contemporary—for example Arial, Verdana, Lucida. There are no flicks and the letters tend to be of uniform line thickness—more blocky.

This is a serif font

This is a sans serif font

There is no hard and fast rule about which is better for ease of reading, especially for text which comes in short line lengths, like prayers and songs. However, some people with dyslexia find it easier to read a sans serif font (and there are fonts designed specifically to help), so in general, choose a sans serif font unless there is a particular reason to pick a serif one.

On screen, the lower resolution can mean that the thinner parts of serif fonts get lost, so that is another reason to choose a sans serif font, which will show up much more clearly.

How Many Fonts?

As a general rule, do not use more than two different fonts in a service. Each font might, however, appear smaller or larger, or in bold or italic forms.

Other Things to Consider

Does the font convey a feel? For instance, Comic Sans looks informal but can also look childish; this might be fine for an All Age service, perhaps, but not for a funeral.

Does the font have a clearly distinguished **bold**? If not, the congregation might not be sure when they are to join in. Be aware that the **bold** might be less clear on screen than it is on paper.

Words for the leader to say.
Words for the congregation to say.

Verdana

Words for the leader to say.
Words for the congregation to say.

Times New Roman

Words for the leader to say.
Words for the congregation to say.

Monotype Corsiva

Words for the leader to say.
Words for the congregation to say.

Comic Sans

Check the *actual* size of the font—all the above examples are the same point size, but they look very different.

Pay particular attention to how the font deals with the letters 'a' and 'g.' The way we are taught to write these at school (*'a'* and *'g'*) is quite different from how they are displayed in many fonts (often 'a' and 'g'). Children, and others who are new to reading, will find the text easiest to read if those letters are closer to how we are taught to handwrite them.

Jargon: Rubric

In the context of corporate worship, a rubric is an instruction—that is, text that tells you what to do, rather than the words to say. It means 'red words' and originates from the days of printed service books in which the instructions were printed in red to make them stand out from the words to be said.

Establishing a House Style

A house style is simply a set of standard settings for different types of text. It makes the service much easier to follow because the use of text is consistent—for instance, bold is always used for the congregation's words; italic always means an instruction which is not to be said.

Standard Conventions	
Headings	**Bigger!**
Leader (or other single voice)	Normal text
Congregation	**Bold**
Instructions (rubrics)	*Italic*
Hymns & songs	Indented
Source/reference	*Italic, small, right-justified*

The easiest way to do this is to set up some styles in your word processor—see above, chapter two.

Rookie Error: Songs in Bold

If your house style is to use bold for the words that everyone joins in with, then it seems logical to put words of songs and hymns in bold... except it just looks odd. Instead, indent the text to make songs and hymns stand out.

Rookie Error: Putting 'All' in Bold

If you consistently use bold for words we all join in with, you will not need to indicate this each time with an 'All'—but if you do need to be more specific, remember that the 'All' is an instruction, so put it in italic, not bold.

Like this:	*All*	**Hear our prayer.**
Not like this:	**All**	**Hear our prayer.**

Basic Rules for Easy Reading

There are various factors that make text easier to read. For more information, see the RNIB website www.rnib.org.uk and their Sight Advice FAQ section. If you want more detailed information about how to create accessible documents, visit the website of the UK Association for Accessible Formats (www.ukaaf.org). Here are some key factors:

Contrast

Black text on a white or yellow background gives the best contrast. On screen it is better to reverse it so that the background is dark and the text light.

However, some people with dyslexia find a pale colour easier than white as a background. The particular colour that works best differs from person to person, but in general white can be the worst, because the contrast is *too* great.

Print Size

A type size of 10 or 11-point will be adequate for some people, but anyone with visual impairment will find it easier if the main text is 12-point or even 14-point on paper (this is often called clear print size). For a large print version, print would normally be 16-point.

On screens the appropriate sizes will be very different—and will depend on whether the screen is being viewed at a distance (as is often the case in church buildings) or closer up (which is more likely if someone is watching on their television, laptop computer, tablet device or phone). Typically, type sizes will need to be 32-point or larger.

- However, do not make the type size *too* big or sentences break up, making them harder to read.
- If space is tight, making just the congregational text bigger (and leaving the leader's text smaller) is a possible compromise.

Space Around Words

Making the page or screen look spacious helps the reader to relax, so do not be tempted to always fill every space with pictures. A spacious-looking page or screen is the visual equivalent of silence in a time of worship.

- The space that matters includes margins, and the space between lines and between blocks of text.
- But do not spread out the lines of one prayer (or one verse of a hymn) too much—work on putting space around the whole *block* of text, not between each line. Keep lines together that belong to each other—for instance, a call and its response or a question and its answer.

Text Format

Justification

Nothing to do with salvation, in this context! Keep text aligned to the left and leave right-hand margins ragged. This is sometimes called left justified, align left or ragged right. This makes text easier and quicker to read, because your eye always knows where to go back to for the next line.

Practical Tip: Song Projection Software

Software designed specifically for projecting songs in worship will usually default to centred text rather than left justified (and some might not give you an option). This is because it looks more balanced on the screen, not because it is easier to read.

Lining Out

For spoken prayers, this means putting in line breaks at points which help with sense and breathing.

- If you are using published liturgical texts, look at how they are laid out in books for guidance on where to put the breaks.

- It is more important for the congregation's text than the leader's (because it helps people keep together when speaking in unison).
- It is especially important for texts displayed in online worship, where it is even harder for worshippers at home to keep in sync with the person leading on screen.
- Note—it takes more space on the page or screen.

Not lined out…	**Almighty God, to whom all hearts are open, all desires known, and from whom no secrets are hidden:**
Lined out…	**Almighty God, to whom all hearts are open, all desires known, and from whom no secrets are hidden:**

Capital Letters

- Never use ALL CAPITALS—it is much harder to read because the word shape is the same for every word (a rectangle) and most of us use word shapes to help us read quickly. We also learn capitals after lower-case letters, so those who are new to reading will be disadvantaged.
- In the era of text messages and tweets, ALL CAPS also tends to look as though you are shouting—so save capitals for when you *do* want them to shout (maybe an ALLELUIA! on Easter Day?).
- Do not use capitals for divine pronouns (His, Your, Thee)—English translations of the Bible do not do so, so we do not need to.
- Do not put a capital letter at the beginning of every line, only at the beginning of a new *sentence* (including in songs and hymns). This makes the sense clearer.

Rookie Error: 'O' or 'Oh'?

The normal rule is to use 'O' (always upper case) when you are addressing someone (this is called the 'vocative O'), and 'oh' (usually lower case, unless it begins a sentence, and followed by a comma) when you are simply expressing a strong feeling.

So: 'O come, all ye faithful' (because you are addressing the faithful), but 'Oh, what needless pain we bear' (because you are not addressing anyone in particular, but simply expressing frustration).

Page Turns or Slide Changes

Try to avoid page turns or slide changes which do any of the following:

- Split a congregational text (such as a confession).
- Separate rubrics from the text to which they relate.
- Separate a call from its response, or a question from its answer.
- Split a verse of a hymn or song.
- Separate a heading from the text to which it relates.

There will always be exceptions to these rules (for instance, sometimes on screen you have to split a confession or creed or the Lord's Prayer across two slides)—but when these occur, use common sense to minimize the impact.

Consistent Versions

Make sure that someone checks that the version of the prayer or song that is going to be on screen or in the service sheet is the same version that the musicians / choir / service leader are using. The internet makes it very easy to find different versions of hymns and songs, but those who put the texts for the service together might not realize that there *are* different versions. The result could be as harmless as a version of a hymn with American spelling or with verses laid out to fit a different tune (such as three eight-line verses, instead of six four-line verses), but it could be as disastrous as someone downloading (and then displaying) all 15 verses of a hymn, of which only 3 or 4 are normally sung.

With hymns, also check whether a traditional version is being used, or one with updated or inclusive language.

Rookie Error: Typing the Lord's Prayer from Memory

No matter how well you think you know the Lord's Prayer, always copy and paste it from a standard version (either online or saved to your computer). Otherwise you will almost certainly end up with a very-nearly-but-not-quite accurate version, probably a hybrid between a modern version and one of the traditional versions (yes, there are more than one!). Even worse, you might miss out a crucial word ('lead us into temptation…'?).

What The Spellcheck Will Not Spot…

Just for fun, a reminder that the spellcheck will not spot every mistake. Here are just a tiny selection of examples from real worship. See if you can spot what the spellcheck missed (tip: in one of them there are *two* errors—once you have seen one, it is easy to miss the second):

- '...the one true and immoral God.'
- '...make your church a bacon of light.'
- '...thou changest not, they compassions they fail now...'
- '...Oh, what needles pain we bear...'
- '...One day soon there'll be fields for the poo.'
- 'The Lord God almighty resigns.'
- 'Though we are many, we are one body, because we all share in one beard.'

Practical Tip: Copy and Paste: Did You Get it All?

When you copy and paste, always check that you have copied the full text you need—it is remarkably easy to miss off the final line of a prayer or hymn (or even the final verse) and not realize until it is too late.

4

Particular Points for Screens

Much of what has already been discussed applies just as much to screens as to paper. However, when you use a screen, there are lots of options that are not possible on paper. This is both opportunity and danger! Pictures, colour, moving images—all these and more become possible. But remember, just because you *can*, it does not mean you *should*.

Images and Words—Practical

If the key point about what is on screen is the words, and enabling people to see them and join in with them, then make sure that nothing else that you do for decoration makes that primary aim more difficult. Putting a picture behind words might look impressive, but it will make it much harder for anyone with visual impairment or with a specific learning difference (like dyslexia) to see the words and make sense of them. Moving pictures behind the words make it doubly difficult. This matters more for prayers and songs than it does for the points of a sermon (for instance), because the text moves on quickly and people need to be able to read the words and join in with them.

If you are using images, keep them separate from the text, or put a box behind the words with a plain background, and put that in front of the picture.

Images and Words—Theological

In addition to the practical issues noted above, the juxtaposition of pictures with words can also produce theological issues. A particular picture can narrow down the interpretation of any words placed alongside it.

If our songs of worship are always accompanied by pictures of worshippers, arms outstretched, silhouetted against a sunset, this will provide a persistent image of what worship looks like—and a very different idea from the same song alongside a picture of a block of flats or a shopping arcade. The Lord's Prayer juxtaposed with a picture of a military tank gives a very different meaning to, 'Deliver us from evil,' or 'Lead us not into temptation,' from that provided by a picture of candles in a church.

> **Rookie Error: The Song Words and the Video Feed**
>
> If you are displaying song words at the same time as a video feed (say, of the worship band), keep the words in a different section of the screen from the pictures. That way the words will be clearer and you avoid the risk of the words obscuring someone's face.

Font

Because the resolution of a screen (even a high-quality one) is not as sharp as print on paper, you generally need to use a blocky font (that is, usually a sans serif one—see chapter three) for text on screen. If you try to use a serif font, the thinner parts of the letters will disappear, making it much harder to read.

Colour

Using a screen means that you have lots more options for the colour of the text. In particular, it means that you can use a dark background and light text, rather than the other way round.

There is always a balance to be struck between clarity and gaudiness. In choosing colours for contrast, make sure you take account of colour blindness and how that might affect your choices. In particular, note that there is a form of blue / yellow colour blindness, which is much less common than the red / green form.

Spoken Words for the Congregation

Bold text does not always make so much difference on screen as it does on paper, so you might have to find other ways to indicate which words are for the congregation to join in with. This might include using a different colour (for instance: white text for the leader; pale yellow for the congregation) and / or indenting the congregation's words.

> **Rookie Error: Colour Matching**
>
> Colours often look different on a computer screen from how they look when projected onto a screen in church. If you are using projectors, make sure you check that before you choose your background and text colours, to ensure that what looks clear on your computer screen does not look washed out or illegible on the screen in church.

Slide Changes

The person who is moving the slides on (whether live, in church, or in a pre-recorded online service) needs to understand the different ways sung and spoken texts operate in worship.

For songs, there are extra aural clues as to what is going on. Often people will recognize the song from the musical introduction, and a choir or music group will give a clear lead, so that if the words of the song are a second or two late, the congregation can usually busk the first few lines if they need to.

With spoken liturgical texts there are not so many clues, and the words might be much less well known, so they need to appear slightly *before* they are needed, not after they are needed. This means you need to change the slide just before we have finished saying the last words on it.

Rookie Error: The Slide Change in the Middle of a Sentence

Make sure slide changes come in sensible places, whether in songs or spoken text. It can be a particular challenge with longer spoken liturgical text, such creeds or prayers. For instance, if you have the Lord's Prayer on screen, it is no good if the slide has to be changed in the middle of a sentence, like this:

> **'...and forgive us our trespasses** [change slide]
>
> **as we forgive those who trespass against us.'**

Not only does it break the sense of the sentence by having an induced pause in the middle, it also breaks the rhythm, which is so important for unison speaking.

Structure, Context and Meaning

When worshippers encounter songs/hymns or spoken texts on paper, they can get a glimpse of the overall shape of the song as they are singing it, or of the service before it even starts. This is more difficult with words on a screen. Because you only see what is currently on the screen, each verse of a hymn, or the line of a song, or the prayer we are currently saying together, is taken out of its wider context.

Displaying a Song One Line at a Time

The most recent shift in displaying worship songs on screen (seen particularly in online worship, but also on screens in church buildings) is to show only one line of the song at a time. This divides up the song even further, and removes any sense of context, flow or shape. It makes lots more room on screen for pictures, or a video feed of the musicians, but it disempowers the congregation even further—they no longer have the chance to see the words they are singing in their context, to understand the flow of the song, or to evaluate its overall message.

To give a sense of the overall shape of the service, one solution is to display a simple diagram of the key elements of the service before you start so that people have an idea of the ground to be covered. Some churches do this informally and orally ('Welcome to our service this morning. We're going to be singing God's praises, praying for the world, picking up on our sermon series on Esther, and then Lesley will be preaching for us.')—why not think about doing it visually too?

Another option is to use some colour code or running title to indicate which section of the service you are in. You could use simple terms like 'Gathering,' 'Word,' 'Prayer' and so on to make clear what is happening in each part of the service.

Punctuation

It is fashionable in graphic design in the wider world to play around with punctuation and even to omit it entirely. Capital letters, commas, full stops, colons—all are routinely omitted to produce a look that is pared-back, simple or edgy.

Whilst this might be appropriate for a church's brand identity, it is very unhelpful when applied to songs and prayers. Punctuation aids understanding and when we leave it out we leave the meaning less clear. When this is about God, that could have serious consequences.

Perhaps the most well-known example of punctuation affecting meaning is from Psalm 23: 'The Lord's my shepherd, I'll not want.' It means, because God is my shepherd I will not lack anything. Without the crucial comma, however, it sounds like God is a shepherd whom you do not want—a very different meaning!

Much software designed for displaying song words deliberately strips out the punctuation to make the text look more attractive on the screen. But if the result is that the meaning is confused, or you cannot even work out when a new sentence is starting, it might be worth putting it back in.

5 Sources and Copyright

Copyright

Copyright in worship texts can seem complicated, and many well-intentioned church or worship leaders continue to break the law week in week out. Thankfully, dealing with copyright relating to songs and hymns has been made much more straightforward (for most, but not all songs and hymns) by the advent of umbrella copyright licensing schemes.

In the UK, any work is copyright if the author is living or died less than seventy years ago. The typography and design of a book is copyright until twenty-five years after publication, which means that until that time you cannot copy the layout of the text from that book without permission.

The church has got used to the idea that many songs and hymns are still copyright, and that musicians, writers and publishers should receive the appropriate payment for the use of their work. Such payment not only fulfils legal requirements, it is also a means of protecting the livelihoods of writers and the investment of publishers in Christian music publishing.

However, payment for the use of copyright liturgical texts is not so well established, nor is there (at present) any umbrella scheme covering several writers or publishers. The best advice is to read carefully the guidance about copyright printed in any book containing prayers or services that you intend to reproduce locally. Unless permission is clearly given for local reproduction for non-commercial use you will need permission in writing from the publisher or copyright holder, which might mean planning ahead and paying a fee.

Church of England Liturgical Texts

Using copyright Church of England texts in local church services is now very simple and straightforward. The basic rule of thumb is that you can use any official Church of England texts in your order of service without applying for permission or paying a fee, as long as the following all apply:

- It is for local use.
- You are not going to sell it.
- You are not making more than 500 copies.

- The order of service (or equivalent) has the name of your church on it (and the date of the service, if it is a one-off).
- It carries an appropriate copyright acknowledgement (see box below).

Fuller details are found in the booklet *A Brief Guide to Liturgical Copyright* (third edition, 2000). This can be downloaded from the Church of England website.

Prayer Book Texts

Copyright in *The Book of Common Prayer* is vested in the Crown and administered by Cambridge University Press. Applications for permission for single use are not required for extracts of up to 500 words. In addition, they have agreed that Prayer Book texts which have been included in *Common Worship* may be reproduced in local editions, subject to the same conditions as *Common Worship* texts.

Do not forget that if you are including other material, with copyright not belonging to the Archbishops' Council, you will need to gain permission from the copyright owner, or clarify that no permission or fee is needed.

Copyright Acknowledgement for Church of England Texts

If you are using material from the Church of England's *Common Worship* services, use this copyright acknowledgement (put it at the end of the service—either the last page or the last slide):

> *Common Worship*, material from which is included in this service,
> is copyright © The Archbishops' Council.

If you wish to give more detail about where the material has come from, remember that *Common Worship* is the generic title and not the title of one book. If you are drawing material from one particular book (for example *Common Worship: Times and Seasons* or *Common Worship: Christian Initiation*), then give that specific information. The title of the main volume (the black book), is *Common Worship: Prayers and Services for the Church of England.*

Local Musical Settings

Authorized and Commended Church of England texts set to music may be used without specific permission or payment of a fee. This is subject to certain conditions: the words must faithfully and accurately follow the official text; the copies must carry the name of the parish and must not be offered for sale or use by others; the document must include a copyright notice. Further details can be found in *A Brief Guide to Liturgical Copyright*.

Bible Passages

For Bible passages, the copyright is held by the publishers of each translation. Some copyright owners allow reproduction, subject to proper acknowledgment, for extracts below a specified word limit. Full details can be found in *A Brief Guide to Liturgical Copyright* and on Bible publishers' websites.

Copyright in Songs, Hymns and Music

Christian Copyright Licensing International

Christian Copyright Licensing International (CCLI) run an umbrella scheme which covers many (but not all) of the most popular modern songs and hymns. Users pay a single annual fee based on the size of congregation for the right to reproduce songs or hymns covered by the scheme. See www.ccli.co.uk

Each church, individual or organization has a unique licence number, which must be included whenever songs covered by the scheme are reproduced on paper or on screen.

> **Rookie Error: Music Copyright**
>
> The standard CCLI licence only gives permission to reproduce the words of the songs, not the music. If your musicians are photocopying music, then you need the additional Music Reproduction Licence (MRL).

CCLI also provide a streaming licence for displaying the words (and, in some circumstances, broadcasting audio) in online worship. Note that this does not *automatically* give you permission to broadcast music videos or professional audio recordings—other conditions might apply.

CCLI provide equivalent licences to cover schools for collective worship and religious services.

ONE LICENSE

ONE LICENSE is another organization offering umbrella copyright permissions via an annual licence. It covers Taizé, Christopher Walker, Bernadette Farrell, Oregon Catholic Press (OCP), GIA Publications Inc and McCrimmons, among many others. Several commonly used songs are not covered by CCLI but are covered by ONE LICENSE, including: 'I the Lord of Sea and Sky (Here I am Lord)'; 'Christ be Our Light'; 'Make Me a Channel of Your Peace.'

> **Practical Tip: Looking for the '©' Symbol?**
>
> You will not find it on the keyboard. Each word processing software is different, but try looking under a menu such as 'Insert' and then select 'Symbol.' From the selection choose the ©. Often it is easiest to try

typing (c) and then a space. Most word processors are clever enough to correct this to © automatically.

Acknowledging Sources

Most copyright schemes require you to acknowledge your sources and the copyright holder (as well as reporting what you have used), even if you do not have to get special permission to reproduce the item. More to the point, it is disrespectful not to do so.

Make sure you leave space for acknowledgments on your order of service, or think about how to include them in your slideshow or online service. They normally come at the end of the service, as this prevents the look of the service being disrupted and cluttered by copyright information. Try to ensure that the copyright and other acknowledgments do not look like the most important part of the service—put them in smaller type and have a house style that makes them easily recognizable.

Rookie Error: Copyright and Pictures

It is tempting to think that if a picture is on the internet, then it must be fine to use it in your online worship, slideshow or order of service. This is not the case. If you are looking for pictures online, set your search engine to filter by usage rights—look for options that are covered by Creative Commons or which allow reuse for non-commercial purposes.

Some websites advertise royalty-free images. This means you do not have to pay a separate fee each time you use them in a new context—it does not necessarily mean they are copyright-free or free of any cost.

Copyright and Acknowledgments on Screen

When a song is split over several slides, you can either give the copyright information at the bottom of every slide or at the end of the song. Your ONE LICENSE or CCLI licence number can be displayed with the song itself, or as a general statement on a final acknowledgments slide.

For liturgical texts there also needs to be an acknowledgment of their source and any relevant copyright information, including that you have permission to use the material. As well as giving the detail of the copyright information, if you are using official material from your denomination you could use your denomination's logo on each slide where you have used official texts, as a way both of acknowledging the source and of indicating your local church's connection with the wider church—effectively saying, 'We haven't just made this prayer up ourselves.'

6 Checklists

A Proofreading Checklist

Use this checklist to help you make sure that the text is right, whether you are using print or screen.

- Run the *spellcheck* one more time. (I know you have done it a dozen times already, but that last-minute change you made is bound to have included a spelling mistake that you missed in your rush.)
- Make sure that the *spellcheck language* is set correctly to either UK English or American English.
- Check for *consistency* of spelling (for example, have you put 'baptise' in one place and 'baptize' in another?). Your spellcheck might allow such inconsistency.
- Check for *hyphens* at the end of lines and remove them (make sure automatic hyphenation is turned off).
- Check for unnecessary *capital letters* (for instance, at the start of a line that is not a new sentence, or for pronouns for God) and take them out.
- Go back and *check your text against a published version* for incidental errors, including unintended variations in punctuation and use of capitals.
- *Read through carefully* when you are not under pressure—even better, start at the end and work to the beginning. The spellcheck will not pick up everything. For instance, '*Left* up your hearts' seems as sensible to the spellcheck as 'Lift up your hearts.'
- Get *someone else* to read through the whole service. They will be more likely to spot errors that have slipped through the net. Good people to ask are the annoying folk who always come up to you after worship to point out the typos and errors in this week's service.

An Order of Service Checklist

This checklist will be particularly useful if you are producing a printed order of service or a songsheet.

- Is the look and feel *appropriate* to its purpose?
- Does the chosen *font* work for this purpose?
- Is the *bold* bold enough? Has congregational text (and *only* congregational text) come out in bold every time it should?
- Check that the text is *aligned left* (ragged right).
- Are congregational texts sensibly *lined out*?
- Check that long lines *break* or *turnover* at sensible places.
- Check *page breaks.* Make sure you have not split a congregational text across a page turn. Check the bottom of pages and columns for single lines left on their own, or for headings or rubrics separated from the text to which they refer.
- Check for *uneven line spacing.* This is sometimes caused during editing when an invisible character (such as a space) set in a larger point size sneaks its way into your text.
- Check for *missing line spaces* between items. This sometimes happens when a page break moves during editing.
- To check other mysterious effects, set your software to display *formatting characters* such as spaces, tabs and returns (see your manual or onscreen Help for details). All might be revealed!
- Check that you have indicated which texts (if any) are to be *sung.*
- Have you thought about how people will find their place (including consideration of *headings, section numbers* and *page numbers*)?
- Are the *margins* wide enough (or are they too wide?), and is there enough white space on each page?
- Have you kept *pairs of call and response* words together, but given space between each pair?
- Are the *headings* clear, but not dominant?
- Could the print size be *larger,* without spoiling other aspects of the design?
- Are there enough / too many *pictures*? Are they appropriate and in the right places?
- Have you included all necessary *instructions* (including about posture)? Are there unnecessary ones you could remove?
- Have you included all the appropriate or necessary *acknowledgments* and *copyright* information?
- Check the *printout*—has your printer cut off the first letters or last letters of sentences on the left or right margins?

Help! I Want to Save Paper

If the service is just too long, and you want to avoid having to use a whole extra page just for three lines, here are some techniques to try:

- Cut out some of the leader's text if the congregation do not need it.
- Reduce the size of the leader's text (try reducing by 0.5 point).
- Reduce the size of other parts of the text.
- Reduce some of the line spacing, possibly just in a few key places.
- Try a different font.

A Screen Checklist

If you are reproducing songs or liturgical texts on screen (in church or online) then this checklist might help.

- Does the text show up clearly against the *background colour*?
- Is any *spoken congregational text* clearly identified (for example, by using bold, indentation, or a different colour)?
- Is the text *clear against its background* (check that it is not on a background consisting of a busy picture or a moving image).
- If lines of songs are appearing in ones or twos, is there enough *context* for them to make sense, and have you divided up the lines in the clearest way?
- Have you included all the appropriate or necessary *acknowledgments* and *copyright* information?

A Final Reminder

We began this booklet by asking why we should bother to worry about all this stuff, which can feel a bit like obsessive detail. This is a good moment to remind ourselves that taking care over this detail is as important as taking care over anything we do in corporate worship:

- It honours God.
- It helps worshippers keep their focus on God.
- It enables as many people to actively participate as possible—including those who have disabilities or particular needs.